Harnessing Y

"Take the Reins, Contr

~ VVIIV"

A guide on how Entrepreneurs can develop a Mindset that will help them take the reins in their lives and businesses. This dynamic guide will help entrepreneurs start, foster, and scale their businesses to win through rightful thinking and implementation.

Do you believe as Walt Disney that "All of our dreams can come true if we have the courage to pursue them?" What thoughts have stopped you from pursuing your dreams or achieving the success you want? *Harnessing Your Thoughts Take the Reins, Control Your Life, and WIN* teaches new and well-established entrepreneurs how to think and develop a winning mindset. Inspired by Napoleon Hill's *Think and Grow Rich,* this easy-to-read guide will teach you:

- How to understand what you are thinking and why
- How to create your ripple effect
- How to elevate your life and business to a new dimension
- How to develop a burning desire and leverage persistence
- How to master your mind and mission
- How to maintain the control you already have and make it better.

Since you are reading this, it means that you are ready to take your life and business to new levels of success.

Lotus Riché, Ph.D.

8X, International Best-Selling Author and
Guinness World Record Holder

Title: Harnessing Your Thoughts

Sub-Title: "Take the Reins, Control Your Life, and WIN"

Author: Lotus Riché, Ph.D.
ISBN: 979-8-9867197-0-9
www.lotusricheignitesyou.com

Critical thinking is a tremendous part of our success in various areas of our lives whether it is personal, spiritual, emotional, or financial. It all starts with what you think about yourself and the world around you. The difference between average people and extremely successful people is the ability to understand what you are thinking, identify why you are thinking it, and harness your thoughts to take control of any situation and Win!

~ Dr. Lotus Riché ~

Acknowledgements

HYT

Where do I begin? There are so many nights and days that I spent researching and gathering my thoughts. As I gathered my thoughts, I leaned on so many magnificent thought leaders, personal friends and family members to present this astonishing masterpiece. I tremendously have benefited from their patience, guidance, support, steadfast loyalty and unwavering love and devotion.

To God, the mother and the father of all creations, I give the highest praise for downloading the message I needed to harness my thoughts during the toughest days of my life when my mother was transitioning.

To Angela Elting, thank you for believing in me. Thank you for the long nights that you suffered beside me to help me write my thoughts and my emotions. For many of those emotions and thoughts, I wasn't ready to share. You gently coached and supported me past my pain. You helped me care for my mother and care for myself at a time when I wanted to give up. You breathed life into me and into this book that will help support and encourage millions of people around the world.

To my staff, you are my family and I thank you for your tireless efforts morning, noon, and night. You persevered through tough times with me. You were with me every step of the way. Whether it was to create something for one of our clients or something for a family member who has passed away, you were there. It is because of your limitless love and patience, support, you helped me to persevere. Each day you helped to jumpstart the energy in me to press on. Somehow you were able to make me laugh when I felt like crying. When I cried, we cried together. Our daily praying and sharing of gratitude helped me cross the finish line.

To my family and friends, my cousins Elizabeth and Corey Ferdinand, my cousins Ongenette and Mike Washington, my cousin Yvonne Taylor Reed, Denise and John Hurst, Dishena McClendon, Dr. Celina Pina-Shemo, the Gang-Gang, the BTBY Family, Dr. Eric Kelly III, Tandra Price and Anshav Jain, thank you for your support. Special thanks go out to my cousin Elizabeth Ferdinand.

To the Miracle Prayer Group, Angela Elting, Kim Jacobs, Margaret Andrews Fournier, Nailah Beraki, Pamela Lue-Hing, Phyllis Weaver, Shirley Murphy, Shirley Powell, Michael Freeland, Charlene Sparks, Dorothy Ross, Hillary Gooden, Mary Cofield, Sharon Fant, when hell was breaking loose all around me, you all came together with pieces of heaven. Thank you for praying with me and holding night vigils, praying with me and over my mother. I don't know what I would have done if I didn't have you all by my side. There was no time of day that I encountered that you weren't there to help. It is a true testament of love and care that you shared. I will be forever grateful.

To Jill Reynolds and Takako Matsudaira, thank you for standing in the gap for me. You know I don't share a lot of my pain, frustration and worries but you were there, checking in to make sure I was ok. Many times, you offered to have sessions with me so I could just purge. You provided guided meditation (Jill)/ Ho'oponopono (Takako) to help me find solace from the pain. You let me know no matter what I was going through, you had my back. Even though you were going through things of your own, you made sure that I knew that you love and care about me.

To Dr. Sabeeta Singh, thank you for being your friend and sister. I remember you checking in on me and always making sure that I was doing well. Thank you for sharing that you are only a plane flight away, and your willingness to drop everything and come on a moment's notice, leaves me speechless.

To Donna Carlock, thank you for being the big sister that I always wanted. Even though you were going through some challenges with your mother being ill and dealing with your own health concerns, you were always there to help me stay the course.

Dedication

HYT

I thank my parents for always allowing me and my siblings to have a say in the decisions that were often made for the family. We were not children who were acted upon, we were a part of the decision and solution to challenges. We can use our own minds and have our own voices stamped into our mind, to know that all people should be afforded the right to think for themselves. They have the opportunity through the richness of life with sound thought placed into positive action to help people, even from the most destitute of existences. People must experience a fighting chance to create and express their brilliance and not go quietly into the graveyard of nothingness. Fly free into the creativity of the uniqueness that the mind can create.

Demolishing mediocrity, elevating consciousness, and knowing that we are not all created equal, we are created superior to the limited thoughts that we may allow others to compare and subject us to. My parents taught me that I can be the orchestrator of my thoughts and the outcome of my dreams crafted into reality for my life. Our thoughts into action create endless possibilities.

Thank you, Elijah and Mary Frances Riché, for showing me that my creativity is endless, I am possible, and all I dare to dream I can create by harnessing my thoughts.

Some of the greatest thought leaders have historically shared that the mind is powerful beyond measure, and I know it is true. Of course, you must believe it since you are reading this book. I heard brilliant minds think alike. Now that we know that we are in great company, let's get to the meat of why we are meeting between the pages of this masterpiece.

It's time to understand ourselves better and live the life we so richly deserve. It all starts with what we are thinking. In the hustle and bustle of the day, there are so many thoughts going through our minds, and nobody is saying, "Stop, I want to get off this ride so I can hear myself think."

Well, enough is enough. Let's ask the question. Seek and ye shall find. Knock and the door will be opened.

Contents

HYT

Foreword

HYT

Dear readers,

It is my honor to introduce to you my dear friend, Dr. Lotus Riché, a remarkable global thought leader and Talk Show Host who has poured her heart and soul into her latest work, "Harnessing Your Thoughts: Take the Reigns, Control your Life, and Win!"

Dr. Riché's ability to connect with individuals from all walks of life is unparalleled. Her latest book is a testament to her dedication and unwavering commitment to empowering others. She has crafted a powerful message that speaks directly to entrepreneurs, showing them how to break free from the shackles of self-doubt and limiting beliefs, and embrace the endless possibilities that await them.

I wholeheartedly endorse Dr. Lotus Riché and highly recommend this life-changing book to anyone looking to take control of their life and unlock their true potential. Her words will inspire and motivate you to pursue your dreams, to step out of your comfort zone, and to strive for greatness.

I am a firm believer that God assigns people to us in life, and I am grateful that God allowed me and Dr. Lotus Riché to cross paths for such a time as this - to impact lives and encourage people to live up to their true potential.

In closing, I urge you to take a chance on this book and allow Dr. Riché to guide you on your journey to success. It will be a decision that you will not regret.

Sincerely,

Kim Jacobs
Host, The Kim Jacobs Show

Preface

HYT

Most people take all types of courses and read self-help books because, deep down, there is a daunting feeling of missing all the joy life has to offer. Many people feel that people around them seem happier, wealthier, and more fulfilled; therefore, they are looking outside of themselves rather than within.

Are you looking for REAL change in your life?

Are you fed up with your circumstances?

Are you ready to discover a fulfilling purpose for your life?

Have you spent a small fortune on self-help improvement books, courses, and coaches that haven't met your expectations?

This guide exists because it's time for you to move into action with the one life you have now. It is a short and life changing read to help you unveil your truths, face them honestly, and change your future. Many People may say that they define their own truth. What if your truth is a lie that you have been told or convinced yourself into believing? You do not get a break. This journey demands the real unadulterated truth. If you are not ready or can't handle the truth, then put this book down and come back when you have the intestinal fortitude... Are you still here? WOW, you have just taken a step forward to freeing yourself.

So many of us look for everyone around us to free us: the Priest, Reverend, Pastor, Doctor, uncle, aunt, sister, brother, father, or mother. Sadly, the only power they have is the power that we energetically give them and none of them can heal the internal struggle festering inside of you. It can lead to heart attack, stroke, and many other diseases.

It takes YOU to turn your life around and this guide is strong and simple to help you do just that. Let's get started.

"Anything in life worth having is worth working for."

~Susan Elizabeth Phillips~

"In this one life in your current body; you are worth having, fighting, crying, staying up late at night, working hard when everyone is asleep, worth sweating, and never regretting. Yes, you are worth it all and more."

~Dr. Lotus Riché~

So, what if nobody ever told you that? I am telling you today. We are walking this journey together. During our journey, I will tell you some things about yourself that you may already know or are learning about yourself for the first time. You might say, Dr. Lotus, how are you going to tell me about myself when you don't even know me?

Here is what I know. You want something better for your life. You want to think better and live better, or you would not have turned the page.

You are tired of not being fulfilled with the information that you have come across in the past, and don't mind challenging yourself to go higher in thought to explore the deep recesses of who you are and where you are going in life. You are not going to just stand on the sideline of life without playing on the field of life. You want in the game; your number is not retired, and your hairdo is not done until you WIN.

During our journey, I will be your cheerleader, your confidant, your mirror, kick you in the pants on some days and all days, encouraging you to never give up.

I will encourage you to revisit sections of this book and do the critical thinking and take the actions needed to get to where you know you deserve to be. Live the fullness of your birthright.

Some days you may feel like crying, DO it! Shouting, DO it! Punching something, DO it! Don't hurt yourself, use a punching bag or pillow. Punching someone in the face, don't do it! We don't want to have to bail you out of jail or see you on the news. Allow yourself to go deep without blaming yourself or someone else or getting stuck in the past and making excuses not to move into your best future.

It's your time, your journey and I am along to walk it with you. So, grab your notebook and a pen, and let's begin.

CHAPTER 1

What Are You Thinking?

HYT

Many people ask themselves why won't this continual chatter in my head stop? Oftentimes people lie down to rest and their body is lying down, but their mind is doing cartwheels like a child at the playground running from the monkey bars to the swings or the slide and never sliding into the sleep their body desperately needs. Then, the one-on-one conversation begins. They ask themselves why am I having these thoughts? This has happened to me many times. It was as if my brain was saying, "Ooh, ooh, if I stop now, I might miss something."

I remember when my mother was transitioning from this life due to her battle with cancer. I was staying in New Jersey with my mother and providing care for her. Not only was I providing care for my mother, but I was also caring for my uncle and cousin, both of whom are special needs. Being home helped to give me strength because it was filled with memories that I could draw on to help my mother remember past events when she had challenges remembering things. Having my best friend and life partner there to support me and other family members was helpful and nerve racking. The bright side of my days was conversations with my mother where she was clear and joyful. Many days as she was slipping away, she would tell me things that almost made my heart stop. One day we were walking through the dining room, she said, "I'm not going to make it this year." I said, "What do you mean?" My mother said, "I am going to die." I was terrified but I tried to hide it. I was often her rock, and I was crumbling. To keep her focus off me and find out what she really wanted, I asked her if she wanted to live. She said, "Yes, but Jesus said no." As you may imagine my heart was aching and my mind was racing, trying everything that I could to help her recover. The one thing that stands out the most is that she had already made her peace and she was ready to go but I wasn't ready to let go. I remember sitting in her room and she and I were talking, and she said, "I'm going to miss you and I said what? Why you say that? She said, "You know what I told you."

I knew what my mother told me, and I was a mess. My hair began to fall out, I had at least three bald patches on my head, and I began to lose pigmentation because of the stress and heartache. I wondered how I was going to stay alive when the woman whom I love more than life itself was saying, "I am dying, and I am going to miss you." I was ready to die with my mother.

I had to pull myself together because I had to live to help my mother move into the next level of life that many of us call heaven. I was exhausted. I looked bad and felt worse than I looked. Running my business, coaching people around the world, speaking on virtual stages while I was going through utter turmoil was the worst time of my life. But I had to keep going. No rest for the weary.

I had to focus and get myself together. I needed rest and one night I was able to take melatonin while my family members cared for my mother. This was what I needed. The next morning, I woke up feeling refreshed, and this book came to me. I had to harness my thoughts, take the reins just like sitting on a horse and pull the reins to guide it in the direction that I needed it to go because I needed to win at helping my mother transition. My mind was racing, I had so much chatter and it had to be silenced. That was the message that I received just as clear as water. Girl, Harness your thoughts.

Have you ever had deafening chatter in your mind, and you just wanted to say SHUT UP!!!

This is one of the first key steps to Harnessing your thoughts.

Let's check in by answering yes or no.

I never have chatter in my mind. _____

I must tell my mind to shut up and it does not work._____

I must tell my mind to shut up and it works.

_____

Like many of you, I had to tell my brain to SHUT UP when I was trying to rest or concentrate on something important. Guess what? It worked and I was relieved until four minutes later when I heard, ooh, ooh, ooh, I almost missed something. There it was all over again. I even started looking at my phone messages.

This is the never-ending chatter that people often hear, and it can almost drive a person crazy. I know that I have had my days. What about you?

The fact of the matter is that this is the norm in many people's lives. According to an article published in 2005 in the *National Science Foundation* about profound research on human thoughts per day, it was discovered that the average person has approximately 12,000 to 60,000 thoughts per day. Of those thousands of thoughts, approximately 80% were negative, and 95% were precisely the same re-occurring thoughts as the previous day. The study substantiates that one of the daily tendencies of one's mind is to focus on negative thoughts and replay them continually. For this reason, we must remove the needle off the record and no longer play the same old sad song that keeps people bound. For the millennials and Gen-X who may have never seen a forty-five or an LP, shall I say remove the track? The long and short is that negative thoughts are pervasive no matter what generation, race, creed, or socio-economical background you come from.

In another surprising study by Leahy in 2005 from Cornell University, scientists found that 85% of what many of us worry about never happens. With the 15% of the worries that did occur, 79% of the subjects revealed that either they could handle the difficulty better than expected or the difficulty taught them a lesson that added significant value to their life.

The conclusion is that 97% of our worries are unsubstantiated and result from an unfounded pessimistic perception. These unsubstantiated worries are a major source of stress, tension, and cause of fatigue for the mind, body, and soul which impacts us on a cellular level and manifests with dis-ease in the body.

For this reason, we must ensure that we are aware of our thoughts and identify which thoughts serve us well and get rid of the ones that take us through proverbial hell. It is a choice. What ARE YOU CHOOSING? Put a check mark next to the statement below that resonates with you.

I am choosing a blissful life.
Most of the time, I choose Hell.

Now, many of us won't openly say that we are choosing hell but here in this book, you can be transparent. When reflecting, you can further understand where you are, why you are there, and how to change it successfully. It starts with honesty 101.

"The worst part of being lied to is knowing that you were not worth the truth."
~Jean-Paul Sartre~

Stop denying and lying. We are groomed to stay in the matrix but even the rabbit knows that "tricks are for kids." It's time to do the grown-up. Look in the mirror now. Go ahead, look in your eyes and speak to your soul where the healing and reality of who you are begins.

Repeat after me:
I deserve honesty in my life.
I am worthy of telling the truth.
I release all lies about me and my life.
Today, I free my mind, body, soul, and future of lies.
From now to eternity, I choose truth.

Many of us want to be millionaires and some of us just want to live a simple happy life not focused on riches or monetary gain but on the richness of peace of mind. Whichever one we elect; it all starts with a worthwhile inventory system no matter how simplistic or elaborate. It begins with a thought. Our thoughts must be analyzed to understand if what we are thinking is serving us or simply distracting us.

"Insight in and of itself is an intellectual comfort. Power in and of itself is a blind force that can destroy as easily as build. It is only when we consciously learn to link power and light that we begin to feel our rightful identities as creative beings."
~ Julia Cameron~

How to Manage Our Mind

HYT

Many of us have thought leaders who we follow to gain wisdom. One of my mentors is Napoleon Hill.

Napoleon Hill started his career teaching courses on selling and advertising, and structuring classes on the principle that a positive attitude, unyielding personal development, and consistent hard work are the keys to success and creating and sustaining riches. In the process of creating his reality, he became a persistent producer of motivational quotes. One of my favorite quotes from Hill about the mind and manifesting is "any idea, plan, or purpose may be placed in the mind through repetition of thought."

In this book, you will use repetition of thought to help you gain the success you need and desire. To think and grow rich, we all must THINK.

Think about what you desire to evolve into, relentlessly, positively, fearlessly sacrificing all false evidence that appears real to you. Let it go straight to hell from whence it came. Remember, the adversary is the creator of all lies.

No, I am not talking about some entity with horns and a pitchfork. The adversary is any opposing force that works against your true ordained path of excellence, and this can include your own negative self-sabotaging thoughts and behaviors that you must free yourself from.

It is without question that when we continually guard our minds as to what we let in and allow to take up space, it helps to mold not only our thoughts, behaviors, and beliefs, but also how we engage with the world. When we avoid stinking thinking, we avoid the negative energies that often stifle the very life of creativity within us.

When we embody our minds with the truth about who we are and who we are becoming, it lifts us to a higher frequency of existence. It allows us to experience and express an empowering vibration. It's like skipping a rock on the ocean and the ripple effect spans as far as the eye can see. This is vibration and as simple as a small rock can have strength and power, so can you. What is the vibration that you want to have?

It starts with harnessing your thoughts to vibrate the effect you want to vibrate in your life each day. It impacts your internal and external relationships with people, animals, money, and every living organism on and off the planet.

We all deserve the best in life. Are you ready to experience the best of life? Circle your answer below.

Yes, I want to experience the best of life.
No, I want to stay the same.

The decision is yours. Decide! Your failure or success starts with your decision. It's a state of mind. You must have a made-up mind either way.

"Whatever your mind can conceive and believe, it can achieve."
~Napoleon Hill~

Chapter 2

It's Ripple Effect Time

HYT

Close your eyes and envision yourself on a nice sunny day at a wonderful lake called _____ (Put your lake's name on the line). It's your special place and it belongs to you. There is peace and quiet, free of distractions and stress. The sun is shining on your face, and you feel great. BREATHE. In your hand, you have a beautiful rock. Feel how smooth it is. What color is your rock? _____ You are going to skip that rock across the top of the lake. Yes, you can skip that rock because this is your lake, and everything here works for your good through the thoughts of your mind. Now breathe and skip your rock. WOW!!! See and feel the ripples as far as the eye can see. This is the energy that you cast into your dreams. A vibration of love, abundance, and your will to thrive. Feel the vibration cast into all good things that gravitate together for sustainable success in all you do. Breathe as you give the breath of life to your dreams.

Note: Be sure to do this exercise even if you must do it repeatedly.

The belief you have is the catalyst to your creating what you desire. It also opens the portals for enhanced abundance. Some people call it faith; you can call it whatever resonates with you. The Bible says that faith is the substance of things hoped for the evidence of things not yet seen. Now that you have cast your positively powerful ripple vibration, write your truth.

What are you hoping for? List three things.

1. _____

2. _____

3. _____

Just know that you are the evidence of the things that you are hoping for are possible and it's your birthright to have all that is ordained to you. Yes, you are a living, breathing miracle every day. You are alive every day after you transition to the next level of existence.

Today, it is time to focus on your mind in the now. Talk to yourself, know yourself, and accept yourself, and most of all, love yourself for who you are and whom you are becoming.

Let's take a moment to reset your mind and come away from all the negative junk that people have told you including yourself.

You are loved by a source greater than yourself.
You are loved by people around you.
You are part of the great "I Am" and you belong.

You are worthy of all greatness.

You are worthy of being heard.
You are worthy of earthly and heavenly riches.

You deserve a great life.
You deserve a stress-free life.
You deserve to be healthy, happy, and whole.

Don't take it from me, do your own work.

Name the God that you believe in_____

If you are atheist, list the energy you believe
in_____

Name two people who love you. List yourself
first, even if you think you don't. You can start
today.
1. Your name_____
2. The other entity who loves you
_____ (this can
be a person or your pet, etc.)

Now that we have that out of the way, we have dispelled some lies that people have told you about love. You are worthy of love, and you are loved.

Remember that Love covers a multitude of sin and opens the doors of creativity to cultivate abundance.

Get positively grounded. Start out each day with love in your heart for yourself and others. No matter what the day may bring, meet it with true love and witness how your mind and your environment change for the better.

Mantra

HYT

Every day and in every way, I bring love along the way. The world around me is loving and great. Every day with love, I celebrate and create.
I welcome all goodness and great health with love.
I welcome abundance with love.
So, it is and so it shall be. Love in and love out.
I operate in the vibration of LOVE.

"Life loves me, and I love life. Because of love, I have more life and love."
~Dr. Lotus Riché~

Chapter 3

You are in Control, Take the Reins

HYT

In the book *Think and Grow Rich*, Napoleon Hill shared that "action is the real measure of intelligence. You become what you think about. To be a star, you must shine your own light, follow your own path, and not worry about darkness, for that is when the stars shine brightest. Whatever your mind can conceive and believe, it can achieve."

Hill decided to cultivate what he would allow himself to think and believe, which molded how he allowed himself to feel about life, people, and circumstances. It is without question that in every circumstance, one thing holds consistently true; we can only control what we do, feel and how we behave. We can only control what we can control. When we take ownership of that, we take control of our own lives, which starts from our thoughts.

It is critical to know what thoughts you hold. Therefore, you should write things down so that you can see yourself in black, white, grey, and in color, to see whatever your truth and the color of your truth is and what it represents: your reality of the life that you are or are not living. It's time for you to live the life that you are designed to live, even if it is outside of the dreams that others are trying to live vicariously through you.

"We only become what we are by the radical and deep-seated refusal of that which others have made of us."
~Jean-Paul Sartre~

Stop allowing people to pull your life strings. No more Pinocchio with the long nose. What you desire for your life is seeking to find you. Often, it is as plain as the nose on your face. Just look right where you are. Know that it is okay to follow your dreams, the ones you first heard whispering in your ear as a child, young adult, or seasoned mature adult over 50.

Let's face it, everyone wants to be in control at some point in their lives. For example, let's look at babies. You know when babies discover taste buds, and you give them tasty apple sauce and they love it. Then, you decide to give them flavorless strained peas, and they blow it out of their mouths. They respond with a surprised look on their faces as if to say, "What just happened? Are you out of your mind? Hey, who changed the baby food?"

Even a baby with no teeth, just gums and taste buds, wants to control what we put on their pallet. They don't even pay the cost to be the boss. Often you pay the cost to be the boss and you can be in control from a positive loving perspective. You must decide and move in the direction that serves you.

Which direction is serving you?

_____

_____

_____

_____

Which direction do you want to go in?

_____

_____

_____

_____

Follow Your Own Path

HYT

Your father and mother are doctors, lawyers, astronauts, teachers, or preachers. Everyone tells you that you should do the same, but your heart is telling you that you should be a singer, dancer, poet, author, or carpenter, building the world one project at a time.

In the words of my oldest sister, Daisy, she says, "Take your own path." I've often wondered how a 5'2" young girl, who never played basketball, managed to get a college scholarship playing basketball. She thought she could and so she did. When others told her she was too short to play, she followed her own path, and you can too.

"There is no reality except in action. Man is nothing else than his plan; he exists only to the

extent that he fulfills himself; he is therefore
nothing else than the ensemble of his acts,
nothing else than his life."
~Jean-Paul Sartre~

Although Mr. Jean says "man," this includes women, all people devoid of sex, creed, or color. It's for you and the burning question that you may face in finding solutions to your challenges. You are the solution to your challenges. Learning how to be and taking action is the key!

What has been stopping you?

_____

_____

_____

_____

_____

Who told you what you should become?

_____

_____

_____

_____

_____

What do you want to become or do? It's not too late.

_____

_____

_____

_____

_____

Now you know what you are thinking about when it comes to what's stopping you. Who has been a hindrance or help in what you want to become or do in your life?

First things first. Stop doing what is stopping you from cultivating the type of life you want.

Whether it is hanging out with people, doing nothing, sleeping all day, procrastinating, not meeting deadlines, being afraid to follow through, etc., you know what it is, so STOP IT!

List it. These are the things that have held me back in the past that I am freeing myself of now because I deserve better. I want better and I am experiencing a better life starting now. I am making a conscious decision now to do so:

_____

_____

_____

_____

_____

_____

_____

Repeat after me:

These are the things that have held me back in the past that I am freeing myself of now. I deserve better, I want better, and I am experiencing a better life starting now because I am making a conscious decision now. I have dominion over my life and evoke the power of source energy to partner with me in the master of my mind as I achieve my dreams. What I conceive, I believe, and I achieve.

I create a better life experience by understanding and working with my mind bridging new horizons through faith in action.

I follow the path that is my own. I am comfortable being uncomfortable to get comfortable. Say it again.

I follow the path that is my own. I am comfortable being uncomfortable to get comfortable.

I am unique.
I am not a cookie cutter.
I enjoy my path and I appreciate myself.
It is for me to understand my path.
I do not wait on the approval or acceptance of others. Great job!

When we see ourselves as the captains of our ships, in our own truths as we define them, we can strategically plot the course of self-discovery and unwavering success. This allows us to see through clear lenses the true hourglass of our own lives. We must program our subconscious morning and night to not be overtaken by social conditioning ruling over our existence.

We are in perpetual creation as we work daily creating what we call life. It's not over until you give up. Winning thoughts water the seeds of expression waiting to sprout up above the ground to catch the rays from the sun as your ideas soak up nutrients that attract bees to pollinate your flowers in your garden of life. Every living thought that you breathe life into wants to live fully without restraint. BREATHE and let your creations live.

Holding nothing back, let's talk to the YOU who was once stifled.

Let's go back to your happiest moment in life. Imagine it and feel the bliss that you were feeling at that moment. Maybe it was a birthday party, Christmas gift, or some event that you said you would never forget. Take the joy of that moment and share that energy with yourself in the present.

Describe how you felt in that moment?

_____

_____

_____

_____

_____

Now, visualize your younger self and let's share your wisdom of today. Write 5 things that you would share with that younger blissful you.

1. _____
2. _____
3. _____
4. _____
5. _____

Why are these things important to you?

_____
_____
_____
_____
_____

What 3 key ideas have changed your life for the better and why?

1. _____

_____

2. _____

_____

3. _____

_____

Chapter 4
Burning Desire and Persistence

HYT

Many of the most profound thought leaders testify that they hold close to their chest the thoughts and guidance of Napoleon Hill, world-famous author of *Think and Grow Rich*.

The book was initially published in 1937 and has sold over 70 million copies. It has helped people experience success all over the world and remains in the conversation of the best business books ever written.

Through wisdom, trial and error, and most importantly, the belief that I deserve the best that life can offer, I have explored many times the life-changing words found in the pages of the *Think and Grow Rich* book and so many other incredibly powerful books which offers the world a process to harness one's thoughts, control one's life, and win.

Just like this book, Hill's book is filled with so many dynamic concepts that have proven throughout history to change the lives of people devoid of where they are from, what spiritual beliefs they have, and without any dependence upon formal education. Everyone who reads the book has an opportunity to change their lives for the better, just like you have while reading this book. Napoleon Hill spent 25 years studying how wealthy people amassed wealth and sustained it. He summarized his 25 years of research in the book; therefore, I will share his 25 years of research and my over 30 years of experience.

Let's get down to infinite wisdom.

In chapter 9 "Persistence" of *Think and Grow Rich*, I learned that there are 6 steps that when we answer and implement truthfully, set us free. Only fear and cowardice can keep you from your truth.

Shake off the symptoms of the fear of criticism. Those symptoms were taught to you. Just like they were taught, you learned and applied them to your life. The endeavors that you do or do not do can be unlearned, you can drop them like a bad habit. Far too often people allow relatives, friends, and society to grab them in a stranglehold of influence where they cannot live their own lives because they fear criticism, being shamed, or being blamed. Huge numbers of people make this mistake, yet you no longer must be in that number. You can break free. Make a choice today to do you!

"Face yourself squarely if you really wish to know who you are and what you are capable of doing. These are the weaknesses which

must be mastered by all who accumulate riches."
~Napoleon Hill~

I further believe that you can achieve more than riches. You can achieve belief in yourself when all else fails, believe in YOU! You can rebuild or never lose the riches of mind, body, soul, and finance.

Without question you can, you will, and you must hold fast to your desire to govern your thoughts. Keep them positive and square in front of you or fall victim to the scratchy whispers of complacency, deception, and misleading thoughts that bombard people every day causing itchy ears to the point that we can't even hear ourselves think soundly.

You must desire not only the ability to take the reigns over what you allow in your ears and mind, but also harness your thoughts to win through correct thinking.

"You must know that all things are possible no matter what the nay-sayers serve you on the silver platter of disbelief, laziness, and self-loathing."
~Dr. Lotus Riché~

I have learned that when you desire something, you have the capability to attain it. Before you can have anything, you must let the flames of desire ignite you to have that thing. Napoleon Hill shares that a burning desire is an initial step towards getting what you want.

I believe that desire is the roaring fire that burns even when we are at rest. That helps us to achieve happiness, great health, and wealth. It is what opens the doors that would otherwise be nailed shut. It is the desire that keeps us moving forward. When we hold to the vision and the state of mind where we see, feel, and believe, we already have what we desire. It makes it easier to obtain whatever we desire on the planet.

It is the fire of desire in your belly that will drive you to persevere. Persistence is the crown jewel that will kick the door off its hinges that once separated you from your hopes and dreams. The Bible said, "We have not because we ask not" (James 4:2).

What is it that you want? You have been placed on notice that you can have it. What are you waiting for? No one can gather the reins for you. Your skin color, level of education, religious affiliation, height, or sexual identity cannot preclude you from the promise.

Only you can place yourself out of reach because of your thoughts that focus on lack and inferiority. ASK FOR WHAT YOU WANT. It is your birthright.

Let's explore the 6 steps I spoke of earlier:

1. Take three deep breaths and clear the mental noise.
2. Fix your mind to exactly what you want. Write it down and breathe life into it.

_____

_____

_____

_____

_____

3. Determine precisely what you are willing to do or give up to accomplish your desire.

_____

_____

4. Choose the date and write it down when you will obtain your desire.

_____

_____

5. Write out a plan/strategy in which to obtain this desire. It can be "I will teach elderly people the skills of survival three days per week." Remember to whom much is given much will be required (Luke 12:48). When we are blessed with talents, wealth, knowledge, and skills, we are responsible for what we have and how we use it or not use it. This is your seed money. You sow and will reap a harvest. Your sowing must come from a full heart of love with peace and love to all with harm to none.

_____

_____

_____

_____

_____

_____

_____

_____

6. Read what you have written down, your desire, and your why. This will help you during the tough times to keep on keeping on. Write your why and keep it simple.

_____

_____

_____

_____

_____

Read this statement twice a day, before bed and when you wake up. Don't limit yourself. You can also say it during the day as a prayer of gratitude.

"Gratitude is the elixir for poverty."
~Dr. Lotus Riché~

It is your time to Believe, Read, and Receive. Ingraining it into your subconscious, you will increase the faith required to achieve your goal. Grasp opportunity when it presents itself. Stop wishing instead of willing your reality.

Don't allow yourself to have impoverished thoughts. Stop compromising with poverty. You are a winner, so think and act like it!

Auto Suggestion: Repeat your goal over and over, from the premise of already having obtained what you desire. For example: Instead of saying, "I <u>want</u> $20 million dollars," say "I <u>have</u> $20 million dollars." Feel the joy of having it and envision what you are doing with it. Who are you helping as a result? Feel the gratitude that comes with having it. Write down why you are grateful and how you feel as a result. When you are frustrated or think that you are not grateful, read it. Reading it will help bring you back to your center. This is part of governing your thoughts and emotions through your own reinforcement of what you know and believe to be true even in difficult times.

_____

_____

_____

_____

_____

_____

_____

_____

Chapter 5

Master Your Mind and Master Your Mission

HYT

So many people are constantly searching for all the shortcuts they can find instead of creating effective plans, whether it is collaborating with someone to help bring to fruition the dreams that they desire. It is unequivocal that the failure to create plans and put them into action because of what other people will think, do, or say is often enemy number one. It messes with our minds, our energy, and sometimes our will to persevere. It gets us off track, focusing on the distractions rather than the one critical component that sets us up for success and longevity. We become a walking, living mess full of stress. We must not pay any mind to the mess and master our mission.

For over 30 years, Master Shi Heng Yi, 35th generation of Shaolin Masters and Headmaster of Shaolin Temple Europe, has studied and practiced the interaction between mind and body. His phenomenal strength lies in the ability to effortlessly combine this knowledge with physical exercises and practice martial arts – kung fu and qigong. He has an astonishing academic background and can teach anywhere of his choosing. However, he prefers to reside at the Shaolin Temple Europe, monastery located in Otterberg, Germany.

I learned valuable lessons from Master Yi. During one of his talks, he shared 5 hindrances to self-mastery. We will explore, implore, exhale, express and grow.

Master Yi described his growing up as an Asian adhering to Asian traditions. This meant when you grow up in an Asian family, unlike in America, it is quite common that Asian children don't argue with their parents and typically either become medical doctors, engineers, or lawyers. Otherwise, their parents will be very unhappy. Having lived in Asia and having an Asian spouse, I am quite familiar with many of the traditions.

Master Yi is one of the people who I admire for following his higher calling. In keeping with Asian tradition, he completed his academic education with two university degrees, an MBA, and various certificates and diplomas as part of his dedication to his parent's desire that he should obtain a means of having a useful toolkit for life. However, throughout his education, he felt something was missing. As he began learning about many different aspects of how plants thrive, what an atom is made from, and how political systems function, somehow the subject of learning something about himself was amiss, which is often the case in many of our lives. Many of us have the need to please with little or no regard for what we desire for ourselves.

When he was introduced to the monastic practices, he was delighted to find out that the main part of the practices was dealing with the exploration and the discovery of self.
He was provided with mental training, the development of behavior combined with physical training in all aspects of what is known as Shaolin Kung-Fu.

Notwithstanding the desires of his parents to go out in society and tackle the world on his own terms, he decided to continue this monastic life and begin learning more about himself. He freed himself from the weight of living his life for his parents, cultural traditions, and self-imposed contracts that were not serving him and began to seek out what is important in his lifetime. Although this undertaking was filled with many challenges, he understood what he deemed as valuable in life. Master Yi began to believe that there was a magic that comes from sharing with others. It often can create an undeniable connection with others as well as oneself on a deeper level that many people do not experience until they tap into enjoying their time with themselves in full expression and love devoid of guilt, blame, or shame. I call it the miracle of finding self, learning to love who you are in a crowded room with a million faces or just staring at yourself face-to-face in the mirror of life. No matter how we do it, we must all do it. Be comfortable in the skin that we are in. Sometimes it's a challenge and I have the solution. Just do it anyway and win!

It does work and it will work if you work it. One main aspect is to find a way and do the things you like to do.

All the aforementioned could only be realized by being truthful with oneself and following one's own path.

He further went on to share his talk on the concept of "High, Higher, Highest," as he reflected on a story shared with him by a master from the Shaolin Temple that I will share with you. However, we will bring it closer to home by putting your name in the blank space below.

A man/woman who we will name _____ (your name) was living close to a mountain. Every day _____ (your name) was thinking: How would it be to climb this huge mountain and what would I observe once I get to the top? So finally, the day came, and _____ (your name) went on the journey.

Arriving at the bottom of the mountain, you met the first of several travelers named Steven and asked, "How did you get up the mountain, and what did you see when you got to the top?"

Steven shared a brief story of his experience while on his path and the view that he experienced once he reached the top and completed his journey. Then, _____ (your name) was thinking, "The way that this traveler described to me sounds very exhausting. Phew, I know I might be in better or worse health, but perhaps I should find another way to climb."

So, you continued to walk at the foot of the mountain until you met the next traveler, Felicia. So once again you asked, "How did you climb up that mountain, and what did you see once you got to the peak?" Felicia shared her story of how she struggled, sweated, and felt fantastic once she got to the top and realized that she could do anything.

However, you were still not determined in which direction and which way you should go.

So, you continued to ask about 40 more travelers. Phew! You were sweaty and parched from talking to so many people and your mind was filled with so many different descriptions of each person's journey to get to the top. When you finished talking to all of them, you finally made up your mind and soul. "Now that so many people have already shared with me their journey, the paths they took and what they saw when they got to the top, I don't need to climb the mountain anymore."

It is very unfortunate that you never explored and never went on the journey for yourself. You only have stories and no true experience. No reality of what works for you: what your journey could have been, what you may have learned about yourself or about life or gratitude, the significance of your path and choosing your own path, and the freedom that it brings along with a sense of completion, closing one chapter successfully while at the threshold of a new adventure.

The moral is that you need to find the most suitable way to climb that mountain. Make up your mind. Make your decision. There is unimaginable information to be shared with words, but it is impossible to share the experience of clarity when you are standing at the top by yourself. Seeing with our own eyes makes all the difference in the world. No one can feel what you feel when you complete your journey. To invest the right effort of climbing the mountain, it's what all the Buddhist practices, Shaolin training, and other spiritual practices are about.

When you climb the mountain, you develop knowledge. You gain clarity of your truth through your experience. Clarity means you see more clearly. The blinders are off. You can have your own interpretation of the experience rather than through the lens of someone else.

When you see plainly, interrelationships become further apparent. When you see unobstructed, there is no need to believe anyone or believe anything second-hand. Seeing plainly means you can discern for yourself which is the suitable direction to take and which decisions you must make to make your goals or objectives start to take shape.

Today, perhaps you've come to realize that you may have often solicited the stories of many different travelers along your journey to include me, but at this crossroad, I can't, nor will I tell you which way to go. You must recognize it, believe in yourself, and decide grounded in confidence, and love for yourself. Decide what is best for your life today and all days to come.

Without a doubt, you will encounter challenges along your journey. You have control over what you allow to stop you from moving forward and climbing that mountain.

You must take the reins and guide yourself on the right path.

At the Shaolin Temple, these obstacles are referred to as "the five hindrances." The five hindrances describe different states of the mind. In those states of the mind, it becomes extremely difficult to see clearly and consequently engage in the right decisions. You can and you must decide. When you harness your thoughts, it will lead you to the correct path for your life.

Master Shi Heng Yi calls the first hindrance "sensual desire." Sensual desire arises in the instant when you are giving your attention to something that provides you with positive emotion. According to Master Yi, this positive emotion can be derived from the five gates of your body: seeing, hearing, smelling, tasting, or feeling. Hence, in your mind, you climb up that mountain.

Subsequently to one mile of walking, you discover a marvelous restaurant encircled by attractive people.

You smell mouthwatering foods and the boundless variety of beverages. You are distracted from your climb even though you have already eaten and even packed a sandwich in your bag. Did I say a sandwich? I mean your favorite one that your mama makes that makes your toes curl when you take a bite.

However, when you follow the temptation and stop and indulge in the food or some other distraction, you have already lost track. When the enticement becomes so strong that you don't want to leave or feel you can't leave that place, the sensual desire has turned into an obsession. In both cases, whether you can or you won't leave, you remain at that place, your vision is obstructed or cloudy and you can't get clarity.

What have you obsessed over which has clouded your vision?

_____

_____

_____

_____

_____

_____

What did you do to overcome it?

_____

_____

_____

_____

_____

If you have not overcome it, don't stand in the shadows of denial. Own it. Now, what are you willing to do to overcome it. What is your game plan and the date you are starting? It takes more than lip service.

_____

_____

_____

_____

_____

According to Master Yi, the second hindrance is "ill-will." This describes the state of the mind that comes because of negative emotions. In that state of the mind, you have a loathing refusal, or simply a dislike against either an object, circumstance or even a person.

Simply put, you are climbing the mountain, and it begins to drizzle lightly, and you dislike rain no matter how lightly it falls. You realize the roads are narrow, and you don't like narrow roads. To cross the river, you need to swim, and you dislike swimming.

Whatever it is that you dislike, it won't make it an enjoyable journey unless you learn to release the ill-will. It's more probable that you will not continue that journey unless you release, breathe, and refocus.

Master Yi initially translated the third hindrance as "laziness and inactivity." "Laziness" means the weight of the body. "Inactivity" means the dullness of the mind. It is characterized by sleepiness, no-motivation, and lack of energy, and frequently can show itself as a state of depression. According to Master Yi, a symbol used in Buddhism defines it as "imprisonment."

You find yourself locked in a cell. It becomes complicated to make any form of mental or physical effort. To continue your path, there is only one option remaining. You must find a way to get out from the dark hole, from that cell that the aforementioned has created for you.

Master Yi called the fourth hindrance "restlessness." It is the state of an unsettled mind. The unsettled mind means your mind cannot settle. You may ask to settle where? Settle from the rollercoaster of thought, internal conflict, and uncertainty.

Settle in the present moment. An unsettled mind either is worrying about the future or reverting to the past and rejecting, judging, or even feeling guilty about an event that happened in your past. It is the equivalent of having a monkey mind, constantly jumping from one tree to another, unable to stay consistent in the present moment. The problem is there is no time to see clearly when in this state of mind.

The last of the five hindrances is "skeptical doubt." It's closely linked to a state of mind, which is founded on indecisiveness. It is very easy in that state of mind to get lost in thoughts. Can I do this? Is this the correct path? What will other people say? What if this? What if that?

In this state, the mind is unable to synchronize with your own actions. The result is that you are disconnecting from the goals and objectives that you previously set for yourself. When the way is filled with significant doubts, more often you will stop instead of moving forward.

Now that we have identified the five hindrances what are you going to do about them? You need to align and structure your life to thwart the hindrances from arising. If you are not successful, you need to use techniques to remove them.

Master Yi said that each of these hindrances is employing a dark cloud on your mind or on the way of you climbing the mountain successfully. Just remember one thing: Just let it drizzle and allow yourself to succeed as you navigate your way.

There is a four-step method to help you remove the hindrances: Recognize, Accept, Investigate, Non-Identity. The first step is to recognize what state of mind you are currently in.

What is your current state of mind?

_____

_____

_____

_____

_____

Next, learn to accept, acknowledge, and allow the situation to be the way it is, or the person to be the way they are. Examine your emotional and mental state, and ask questions:

Why did it come up?

_____

_____

_____

_____

_____

_____

What is the consequence if I remain in that state?

_____

_____

_____

_____

_____

Lastly, non-identification means it is practice.

Let's practice. Repeat after me:

I am not the body.
I am not the mind.
I am not my emotion.
I can see all these characteristics of me.

All our lives are unique. We are of great service when we refrain from copying the path from someone else.

To bring meaning to your life and bring value into your life, you need to learn and master yourself, and do not allow the hindrances to halt you.

If you choose to climb that path to clarity, I would be delighted to meet and congratulate you at the top.

As you reflect, remember that practice does not make perfect, rather it makes you prepared to flow through difficult challenges. Remember my words: patience, persistence, poise, pace, plan, and persevere.

1. Be <u>patient</u> with yourself and others no matter the situation.
2. Be <u>persistent</u> and stay focused no matter the distraction or temptation to deviate from your path.
3. Maintain your <u>poise</u>, stay composed and self-assured.

4. Stay at your <u>pace</u> and do not mirror someone else's pace which does not serve you. It is your rhythm, the very cadence that you use to walk. Maintain a high frequency.
5. Have your <u>plan</u> before you. Review it and live it.
6. Continue to do more than survive. You must thrive and <u>persevere</u>.

According to Dennis Kimbro, "There are no open doors to the temples of success... You must remember that it is you who creates your own opportunities—fate, luck or chance." Take the chance, determine your own fate by harnessing your own thoughts.

Chapter 6

How to Maintain Your Control and Make it Better

HYT

We have come a long way together during this journey of harnessing your thoughts, taking the reins of your life, business and any endeavor you set your mind to. You have been given the tools to help you use your thoughts to win on every level and overcome challenges that may have knocked you off your feet or punched the wind out of you. The power is in your thoughts, and you must exercise your mind and tame your thoughts by maintaining the control that you either enhanced or cultivated during this journey.

Our journey is not over. There are more days ahead and challenges that may rise. There are mentees and mentors who you will connect with, and this book is a tool and a companion that you can use for the rest of your life. Reflect frequently. It will support you, inspire you and give you a recall to help you and others you know and care about.

For the days ahead, continue to ask yourself the question that so many people are afraid of asking. Many people walk aimlessly devoid of asking the one question that will help set them free. Empower them to be in control of what they think. Establish control over the reins of their lives. Remember you are not them. You are a person that harnesses your thoughts and moves into action to pull the reins and navigate your path with success.

When you face challenges, feel afraid, are doubting yourself or comparing your value and self-worth to others, STOP it!
Recenter yourself. Pull the reins in and navigate the course.

Ask yourself: What am I thinking and why? Write it down so that you can see it clearly before you. This will help you harness your thoughts.

Here's a technique you can use inspired by the 3-6-9 Method, popularized by Nicola Tesla.

- Get a piece of paper and write down what you want to manifest. Writing it down will super boost your intention. Remember to write in present tense, in the now.
- Describe how you feel with an adjective, such as great, amazing, etc.
- Visualize yourself in your moment as it has occurred in your life. Refer to page 39.
- Remove all doubts and beliefs and know that it's coming. Have faith. Keep your vibration high.
- Hold to that thought for 17 seconds. According to Abraham Hicks, the 17 seconds that you focus on is critical in the

endeavor to ignite the vibration of what you are manifesting.

- Don't be distracted. Refer to page 71. Stay the course. You're almost there. You got this. Now turn your dream into your reality.

Sample manifestation:

- I am happy and grateful that my products and services positively help motivate people around the world.
- I am grateful that I make $25,000 a month training and speaking to people worldwide.

Remember don't just think. You must FEEL. During this journey through this book, you were speaking to me, the universe, God, the source, and most importantly to yourself. You see, I know I said I would be on this journey with you, and we are still on this wonderful journey with a better sense of understanding.

What you are thinking and ask yourself what do you really want?

Do you want to be free? Well, you should be feeling some weight lifted off your shoulders. When you opened this book and began to turn the pages, you were on the road to freedom. On the road to change and on the road to knowing the real you who you must allow yourself to be and earnestly invest in mind, body, and soul.

Congratulations on your commitment to read and embrace this book. Furthermore, take action in your life and all your endeavors. Now it's time to go back over your answers, notes, and thoughts to review what you have revealed about yourself.

No need to fear or be bashful because you stand, live, and breathe in your truth. The truth is that you have harnessed your thoughts, took the reins of your life and you are a WINNER. Keep striving and know that the best is yet to come.

<u>Note of thanks to you</u>

Thank you for taking time to stop in the store or online to invest in yourself by acquiring this book.

It is my desire that everyone can live the incredible lives we were designed to live through positive thoughts and action.

Today you took action, and you now have tools that will work for you if you "plan your work and work your plan" as my friend Coach Pamela Lue-Hing says.

"For what it's worth, it's never too late, or in my case too early, to be whoever you want to be. There's no time limit."
~F. Scott Fitzgerald~

Use this book frequently. This is your guide and companion.

Give a copy of this book to someone you know and care about. They can serve as an accountability partner for you.

The tools and strategies are fluid, and you will learn new things each time you revisit the chapters.

Be sure to connect with me and get my other great book _Money Does Grow on Trees: The Process of Seed Money and How to Use It_.

Be sure to share your progress and how this book has touched your life.
lotus@lotusricheignitesyou.com
_+1 855-544-4574_

Be Blessed, Be Free
Harness Your Thoughts,
Take the Reins, Control Your Life, and WIN!

References

Cameron, Julia, 2016. *The Artist's Way: A Spiritual Path to Higher Creativity*. 25th anniversary edition. New York, New York: TarcherPerigee.

Fitzgerald, F. Scott, 2008. *The Curious Case of Benjamin Button*. London, England: Penguin Classics.

Hill, Napoleon, 2007. *Think and Grow Rich*. New York, New York: Tarcher.

Kimbro, Dennis, & Hill, Napoleon, 1991. *Think and Grow Rich: A Black Choice*. New York: Fawcett Columbine.

Lue-Hing, Pamela, 2021. Personal conversation with Dr. Pamela Lue-Hing.

Phillips, Susan Elizabeth, n.d. "Susan Elizabeth Phillips quotes."

https://quotepark.com/authors/susan-
elizabeth-phillips/. Accessed 22 June 2022.

Sartre, Jean-Paul, 2007. *Existentialism is a
Humanism*. Translated by Carol Macomber.
New Haven, CT: Yale University Press.

Scott, Devin, 2022, July 5. *Think and Grow Rich
Book Review*.
https://www.delawareinc.com/blog/think-
and-grow-rich-book-review/. Accessed 4 April
2022.

Wong, Kenneth, 2022. "How to Manifest in 17
Seconds by Abraham Hicks."
https://millennial-grind.com/how-to-manifest-
in-17-seconds-in-5-steps/. Accessed 7 May
2022.

Yi, Shi Heng, 2020. *The 5 Hindrances to Self-
Mastery*
[Video] TED Conferences.

Made in the USA
Columbia, SC
19 July 2024

38452239R00054